Life in Line

Monthly management for messy minds

Georgia Worthington

May you touch dragonflies and stars,

dance with fairies and talk to the moon.

Unknown

Be kind to
yourself
and others.

With self belief

nothing is impossible.

For Mum and Dad

Hey, you.

Yes, you.

You really are a beautiful soul.

Have you told yourself that lately?

I can hear your mind speaking to you.

I know you can hear it too.

But are you listening?

Most of us don't say these words to ourselves even though we may say them to others throughout our day. This journal is a reminder to you to spend small moments throughout the day, reflecting on you. Just you and how you might be feeling.

You spend so much time giving to others – your partner, parents, children, neighbour's, strangers, work mates. You smile as you listen and bring happiness and kindness into their worlds.

But what about your world?

When was the last time you checked in and listened to you?

When was the last time you reflected on who you are and your needs?

Expressing gratitude and reflecting on who you are, setting daily intentions, is not being selfish. It's keeping your cup full. It's daily self-care that educates the heart, your heart, for total alignment – mind, body and soul.

Give yourself permission

to be your own light

before you shine

on others.

This journal provides a safe space for you to record and reflect on your daily habits and the amount of self care you give yourself over 31 days. Most of all, it's in tick and flick form, purposefully built this way so it can be done when having a cup of tea, and also, when viewed, gives an overall evaluation in one quick glance.

Take these moments just for you.
Reflect on your day.
Can you see patterns emerging?
Our days feed our souls.
How is yours feeling right now?
Should you be a little kinder to yourself?
Is your mind and your soul
in total alignment
with your heart?

Love you

All of you

For all time

Love your mistakes.

Love your successes.

Love your weaknesses.

Love your strengths.

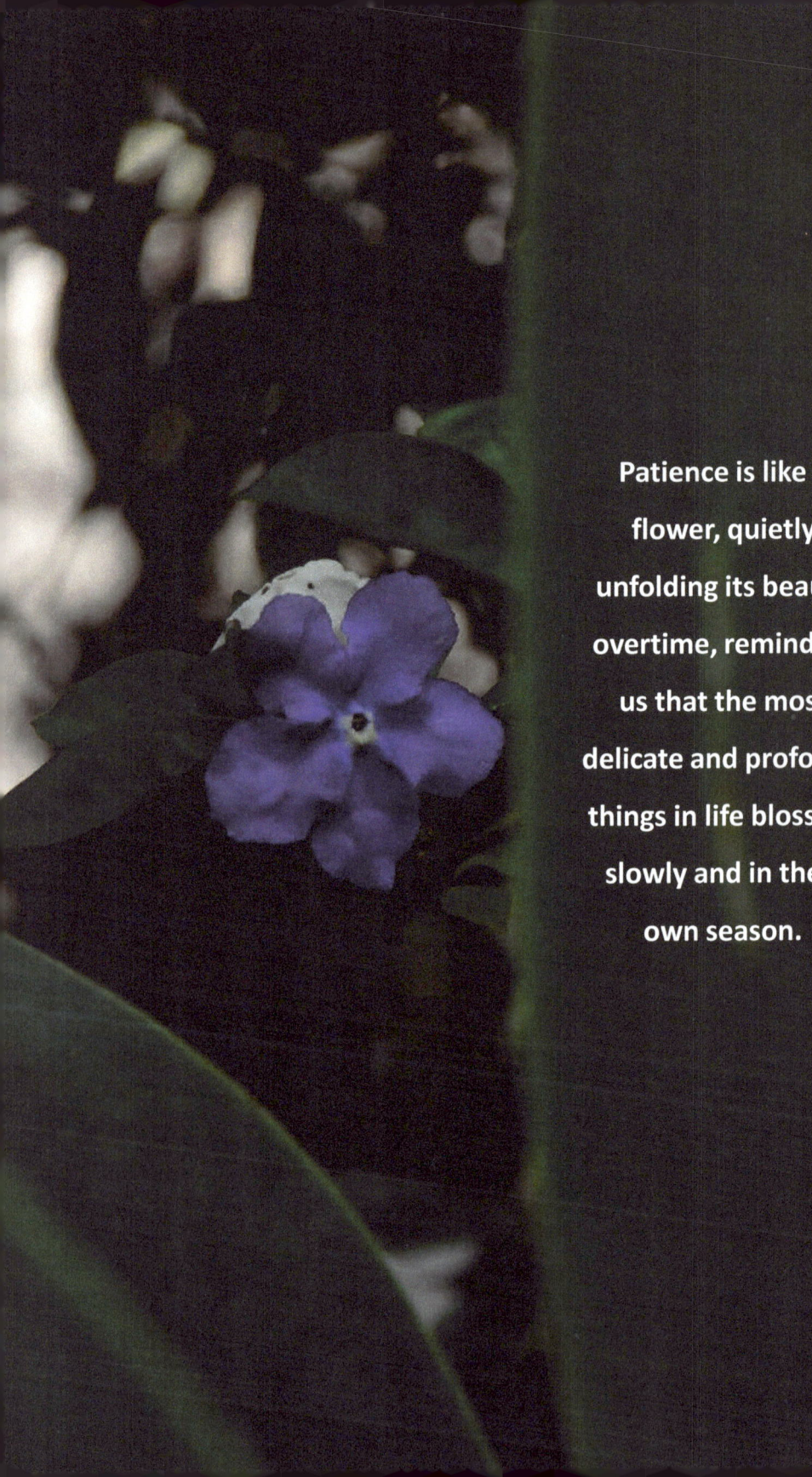

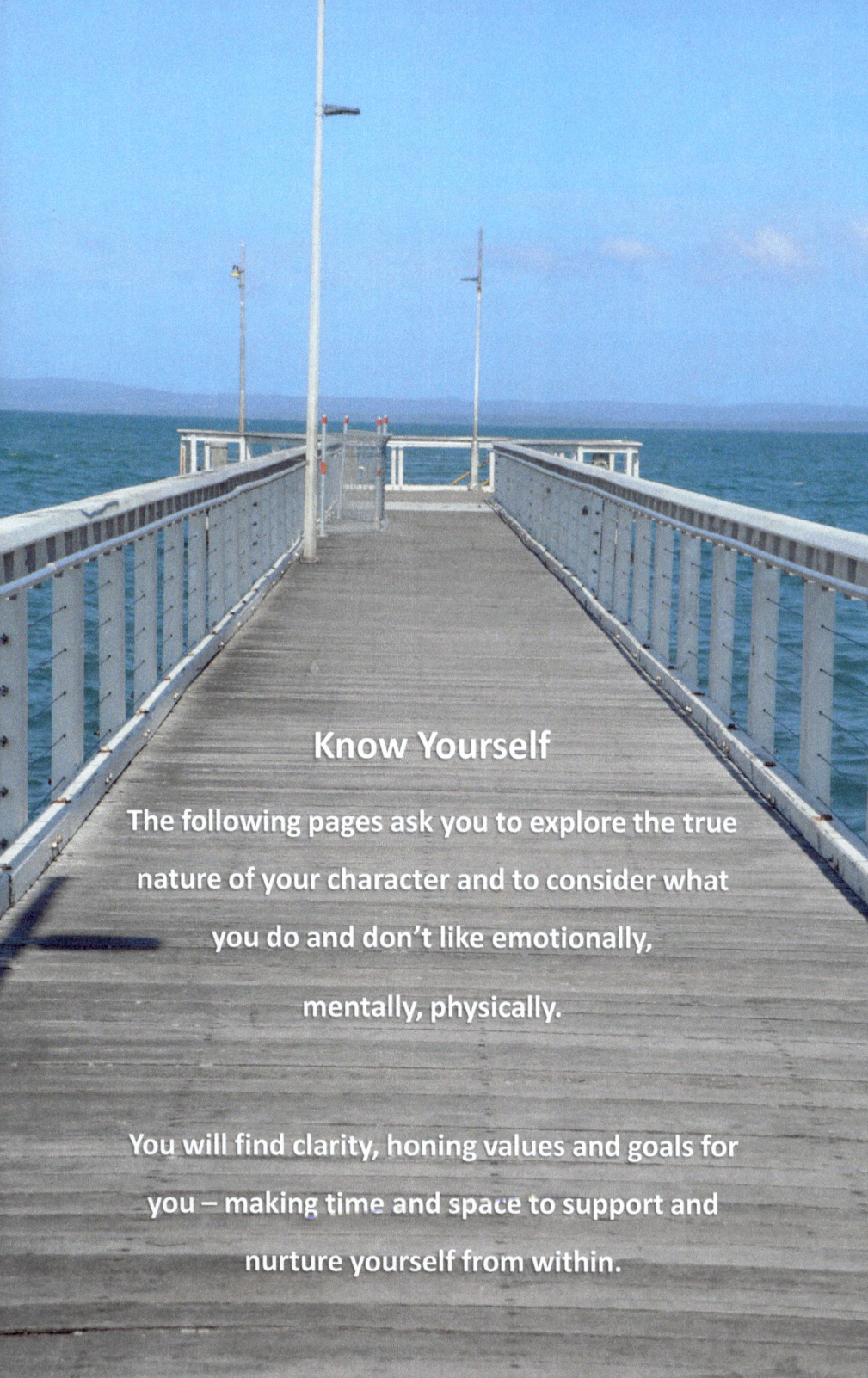

Know Yourself

The following pages ask you to explore the true nature of your character and to consider what you do and don't like emotionally, mentally, physically.

You will find clarity, honing values and goals for you – making time and space to support and nurture yourself from within.

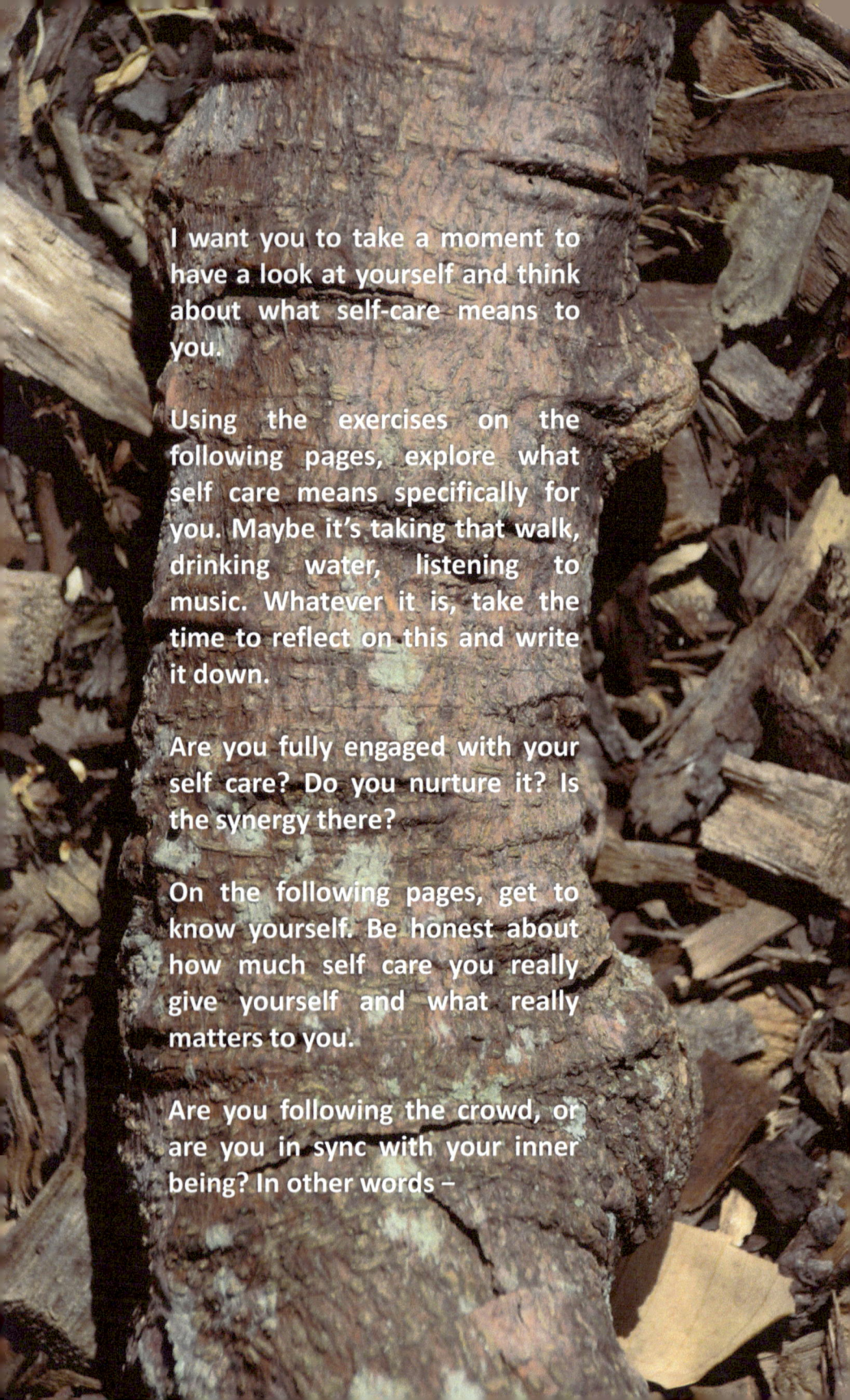

I want you to take a moment to have a look at yourself and think about what self-care means to you.

Using the exercises on the following pages, explore what self care means specifically for you. Maybe it's taking that walk, drinking water, listening to music. Whatever it is, take the time to reflect on this and write it down.

Are you fully engaged with your self care? Do you nurture it? Is the synergy there?

On the following pages, get to know yourself. Be honest about how much self care you really give yourself and what really matters to you.

Are you following the crowd, or are you in sync with your inner being? In other words –

What does self care look like to you?

Think about who are you? Do you really know yourself well enough to care properly for yourself?

What do YOU think of YOU?

Write down 5 words that you feel describes you. Don't overthink it. Write down what comes immediately to mind. Be honest. Don't write down what you think others may think of you.

You need to know what YOU think of YOU.

1. _____
   _____

2. _____
   _____

3. _____
   _____

4. _____
   _____

5. _____
   _____

Using these five words, write down what each of them mean to you. Once again, don't overthink it. What is your gut telling you?

1. _____

2. _____

3. _____

4. _____
_____
_____
_____
_____

5. _____
_____
_____
_____
_____

Use the following pages to write down your thoughts, ideas, beliefs, values about what you know about self care and be honest with yourself about how much you practice it.

Honesty is key.

If only I was...

It's important to accept and love the person you are. Go back to the five words you came up with that you think describe you. Note below any character traits you see. Are you feeling good about you or is there space for growth? What is it that you dislike about yourself and why? Write down your thoughts on how you may be able to change these beliefs about yourself that will enable positive thinking.

_____

_____

_____

_____

_____

_____

_____

_____

_____

Knowledge speaks

Wisdom listens

Anon

The first page sets your daily intention for the beginning of each day.

The second page is a daily reflection to be filled out at the end of the day.

Let's begin...

Daily Intention   Day 1

It is my intention today to:

_____

_____

How did I feel when I first woke today? Sluggish, tired, negative, grumpy, happy, positive.

_____

_____

How did I sleep? How many hours did I sleep for?

_____

_____

Did I dream? Nightmare? Neither?

_____

_____

Breakfast	
Lunch	
Dinner	
In-between	
drinks	

Will I do any exercise, or will I be a couch potato?

_____

What other activities will I do? Cook, clean, play with my animals, be social, create, meditate, give to others, me time, learn…

_____

Daily Reflection

Today I physically feel?

__ rested __stressed __sluggish

__ strong __relaxed __ weak

__energized __tired __positive

What did I do for others today?
_____
_____

What did I do for me today?
_____
_____

How do I feel emotionally?
_____
_____

Is my cup half full or half empty?
_____
_____

My affirmation for tomorrow

_____
_____
_____
_____
_____

Daily Intention   Day 2

It is my intention today to:

_____

_____

How did I feel when I first woke today? Sluggish, tired, negative, grumpy, happy, positive.

_____

_____

How did I sleep? How many hours did I sleep for?

_____

_____

Did I dream? Nightmare? Neither?

_____

_____

Breakfast	
Lunch	
Dinner	
In-between	
drinks	

Will I do any exercise, or will I be a couch potato?

_____

What other activities will I do? Cook, clean, play with my animals, be social, create, meditate, give to others, me time, learn...

_____

Daily Reflection

Today I physically feel?

__ rested   __ stressed   __ sluggish

__ strong   __ relaxed   __ weak

__ energized   __ tired   __ positive

What did I do for others today?
_____
_____

What did I do for me today?
_____
_____

How do I feel emotionally?
_____
_____

Is my cup half full or half empty?
_____
_____

My affirmation for tomorrow

_____

_____

_____

_____

_____

Daily Intention   Day 3

It is my intention today to:

_____
_____

How did I feel when I first woke today? Sluggish, tired, negative, grumpy, happy, positive.

_____
_____

How did I sleep? How many hours did I sleep for?
_____
_____

Did I dream? Nightmare? Neither?
_____
_____

Breakfast	
Lunch	
Dinner	
In-between	
drinks	

Will I do any exercise, or will I be a couch potato?

_____

What other activities will I do? Cook, clean, play with my animals, be social, create, meditate, give to others, me time, learn…

_____

Daily Reflection

Today I physically feel?

__ rested   __stressed   __sluggish

__ strong   __relaxed   __ weak

__energized   __tired   __positive

What did I do for others today?
_____
_____

What did I do for me today?
_____
_____

How do I feel emotionally?
_____
_____

Is my cup half full or half empty?
_____
_____

My affirmation for tomorrow

_____

_____

_____

_____

_____

Daily Intention   Day 4

It is my intention today to:

_____
_____

How did I feel when I first woke today? Sluggish, tired, negative, grumpy, happy, positive.

_____
_____

How did I sleep? How many hours did I sleep for?
_____
_____

Did I dream? Nightmare? Neither?
_____
_____

Breakfast	
Lunch	
Dinner	
In-between	
drinks	

Will I do any exercise, or will I be a couch potato?

_____

What other activities will I do? Cook, clean, play with my animals, be social, create, meditate, give to others, me time, learn…

_____

Daily Reflection

Today I physically feel?

__ rested   __stressed   __sluggish

__ strong   __relaxed   __ weak

__energized   __tired   __positive

What did I do for others today?
_____
_____

What did I do for me today?
_____
_____

How do I feel emotionally?
_____
_____

Is my cup half full or half empty?
_____
_____

My affirmation for tomorrow

_____
_____
_____
_____
_____

Daily Intention   Day 5

It is my intention today to:

_____
_____

How did I feel when I first woke today? Sluggish, tired, negative, grumpy, happy, positive.

_____
_____

How did I sleep? How many hours did I sleep for?
_____
_____

Did I dream? Nightmare? Neither?
_____
_____

Breakfast	
Lunch	
Dinner	
In-between drinks	

Will I do any exercise, or will I be a couch potato?

_____

What other activities will I do? Cook, clean, play with my animals, be social, create, meditate, give to others, me time, learn…

_____

Daily Reflection

Today I physically feel?

__ rested   __stressed   __sluggish

__ strong   __relaxed   __ weak

__energized   __tired   __positive

What did I do for others today?
_____
_____

What did I do for me today?
_____
_____

How do I feel emotionally?
_____
_____

Is my cup half full or half empty?
_____
_____

My affirmation for tomorrow

_____

_____

_____

_____

Daily Intention   Day 6

It is my intention today to:

_____
_____

How did I feel when I first woke today? Sluggish, tired, negative, grumpy, happy, positive.

_____
_____

How did I sleep? How many hours did I sleep for?
_____
_____

Did I dream? Nightmare? Neither?
_____
_____

Breakfast	
Lunch	
Dinner	
In-between	
drinks	

Will I do any exercise, or will I be a couch potato?

_____

What other activities will I do? Cook, clean, play with my animals, be social, create, meditate, give to others, me time, learn…

_____

Daily Reflection

Today I physically feel?

___ rested   ___ stressed   ___ sluggish

___ strong   ___ relaxed   ___ weak

___ energized   ___ tired   ___ positive

What did I do for others today?
_____
_____

What did I do for me today?
_____
_____

How do I feel emotionally?
_____
_____

Is my cup half full or half empty?
_____
_____

My affirmation for tomorrow

_____
_____
_____
_____

Daily Intention   Day 7

It is my intention today to:

_____
_____

How did I feel when I first woke today? Sluggish, tired, negative, grumpy, happy, positive.

_____
_____

How did I sleep? How many hours did I sleep for?

_____

Did I dream? Nightmare? Neither?

_____

What will I eat today?

Breakfast	
Lunch	
Dinner	
In-between	
drinks	

Will I do any exercise, or will I be a couch potato?

_____

What other activities will I do? Cook, clean, play with my animals, be social, create, meditate, give to others, me time, learn…

_____

Daily Reflection

Today I physically feel?

__ rested   __stressed   __sluggish

__ strong   __relaxed   __ weak

__energized   __tired   __positive

What did I do for others today?

_____

_____

What did I do for me today?

_____

_____

How do I feel emotionally?

_____

_____

Is my cup half full or half empty?

_____

_____

My affirmation for tomorrow

_____

_____

_____

_____

Daily Intention   Day 8

It is my intention today to:

_____
_____

How did I feel when I first woke today? Sluggish, tired, negative, grumpy, happy, positive.

_____
_____

How did I sleep? How many hours did I sleep for?
_____
_____

Did I dream? Nightmare? Neither?
_____
_____

Breakfast	
Lunch	
Dinner	
In-between	
drinks	

Will I do any exercise, or will I be a couch potato?

_____

What other activities will I do? Cook, clean, play with my animals, be social, create, meditate, give to others, me time, learn...

_____

Daily Reflection

Today I physically feel?

__ rested   __stressed   __sluggish

__ strong   __relaxed   __ weak

__energized   __tired   __positive

What did I do for others today?
_____
_____

What did I do for me today?
_____
_____

How do I feel emotionally?
_____
_____

Is my cup half full or half empty?
_____
_____

My affirmation for tomorrow

_____
_____
_____
_____
_____

Daily Intention   Day 9

It is my intention today to:

_____
_____

How did I feel when I first woke today? Sluggish, tired, negative, grumpy, happy, positive.

_____
_____

How did I sleep? How many hours did I sleep for?
_____
_____

Did I dream? Nightmare? Neither?
_____
_____

Breakfast	
Lunch	
Dinner	
In-between	
drinks	

Will I do any exercise, or will I be a couch potato?

_____

What other activities will I do? Cook, clean, play with my animals, be social, create, meditate, give to others, me time, learn…

_____

Daily Reflection

Today I physically feel?

__ rested   __stressed   __sluggish

__ strong   __relaxed   __ weak

__energized   __tired   __positive

What did I do for others today?
_____
_____

What did I do for me today?
_____
_____

How do I feel emotionally?
_____
_____

Is my cup half full or half empty?
_____
_____

My affirmation for tomorrow

_____
_____
_____
_____
_____

Daily Intention   Day 10

It is my intention today to:

_____
_____

How did I feel when I first woke today? Sluggish, tired, negative, grumpy, happy, positive.

_____
_____

How did I sleep? How many hours did I sleep for?

_____
_____

Did I dream? Nightmare? Neither?

_____
_____

Breakfast	
Lunch	
Dinner	
In-between	
drinks	

Will I do any exercise, or will I be a couch potato?

_____

What other activities will I do? Cook, clean, play with my animals, be social, create, meditate, give to others, me time, learn...

_____

Daily Reflection

Today I physically feel?

__ rested   __stressed   __sluggish

__ strong   __relaxed   __ weak

__energized   __tired   __positive

What did I do for others today?
_____
_____

What did I do for me today?
_____
_____

How do I feel emotionally?
_____
_____

Is my cup half full or half empty?
_____
_____

My affirmation for tomorrow

_____

_____

_____

_____

_____

Daily Intention   Day 11

It is my intention today to:

_____
_____

How did I feel when I first woke today? Sluggish, tired, negative, grumpy, happy, positive.

_____
_____

How did I sleep? How many hours did I sleep for?
_____
_____

Did I dream? Nightmare? Neither?
_____
_____

Breakfast	
Lunch	
Dinner	
In-between	
drinks	

Will I do any exercise, or will I be a couch potato?

_____

What other activities will I do? Cook, clean, play with my animals, be social, create, meditate, give to others, me time, learn…

_____

Daily Reflection

Today I physically feel?

__ rested   __stressed   __sluggish

__ strong   __relaxed   __ weak

__energized   __tired   __positive

What did I do for others today?
_____
_____

What did I do for me today?
_____
_____

How do I feel emotionally?
_____
_____

Is my cup half full or half empty?
_____
_____

My affirmation for tomorrow

_____
_____
_____
_____
_____

Daily Intention   Day 12

It is my intention today to:

_____
_____

How did I feel when I first woke today? Sluggish, tired, negative, grumpy, happy, positive.

_____
_____

How did I sleep? How many hours did I sleep for?

_____
_____

Did I dream? Nightmare? Neither?

_____
_____

Breakfast	
Lunch	
Dinner	
In-between	
drinks	

Will I do any exercise, or will I be a couch potato?

_____

What other activities will I do? Cook, clean, play with my animals, be social, create, meditate, give to others, me time, learn...

_____

Daily Reflection

Today I physically feel?

__ rested   __stressed   __sluggish

__ strong   __relaxed   __ weak

__energized   __tired   __positive

What did I do for others today?
_____
_____

What did I do for me today?
_____
_____

How do I feel emotionally?
_____
_____

Is my cup half full or half empty?
_____
_____

My affirmation for tomorrow

_____
_____
_____
_____
_____

Daily Intention   Day 13

It is my intention today to:

_____
_____

How did I feel when I first woke today? Sluggish, tired, negative, grumpy, happy, positive.

_____
_____

How did I sleep? How many hours did I sleep for?
_____
_____

Did I dream? Nightmare? Neither?
_____
_____

Breakfast	
Lunch	
Dinner	
In-between	
drinks	

Will I do any exercise, or will I be a couch potato?

_____

What other activities will I do? Cook, clean, play with my animals, be social, create, meditate, give to others, me time, learn…

_____

Daily Reflection

Today I physically feel?

__ rested __stressed __sluggish

__ strong __relaxed __ weak

__energized __tired __positive

What did I do for others today?
_____
_____

What did I do for me today?
_____
_____

How do I feel emotionally?
_____
_____

Is my cup half full or half empty?
_____
_____

My affirmation for tomorrow

_____

_____

_____

_____

_____

Daily Intention   Day 14

It is my intention today to:

_____

_____

How did I feel when I first woke today? Sluggish, tired, negative, grumpy, happy, positive.

_____

_____

How did I sleep? How many hours did I sleep for?

_____

_____

Did I dream? Nightmare? Neither?

_____

_____

Breakfast	
Lunch	
Dinner	
In-between	
drinks	

Will I do any exercise, or will I be a couch potato?

_____

What other activities will I do? Cook, clean, play with my animals, be social, create, meditate, give to others, me time, learn…

_____

Daily Reflection

Today I physically feel?

___ rested ___ stressed ___ sluggish

___ strong ___ relaxed ___ weak

___ energized ___ tired ___ positive

What did I do for others today?
_____
_____

What did I do for me today?
_____
_____

How do I feel emotionally?
_____
_____

Is my cup half full or half empty?
_____
_____

My affirmation for tomorrow
_____
_____
_____
_____
_____

Chickens may cluck, peek and fluff about with no grand plans, but they remind us that sometimes it's okay to keep life simple, scratch around for joy and enjoy the little things.

Persitence (and a little messiness) can create something truly remarkable in the end.

Daily Intention   Day 15

It is my intention today to:

_____

_____

How did I feel when I first woke today? Sluggish, tired, negative, grumpy, happy, positive.

_____

_____

How did I sleep? How many hours did I sleep for?

_____

_____

Did I dream? Nightmare? Neither?

_____

_____

Breakfast	
Lunch	
Dinner	
In-between	
drinks	

Will I do any exercise, or will I be a couch potato?

_____

What other activities will I do? Cook, clean, play with my animals, be social, create, meditate, give to others, me time, learn…

_____

Daily Reflection

Today I physically feel?

__ rested　　　　　__stressed　　　　　__sluggish

__ strong　　　　　__relaxed　　　　　__ weak

__energized　　　　__tired　　　　　　__positive

What did I do for others today?
_____
_____

What did I do for me today?
_____
_____

How do I feel emotionally?
_____
_____

Is my cup half full or half empty?
_____
_____

My affirmation for tomorrow

_____
_____
_____
_____
_____

Daily Intention   Day 16

It is my intention today to:

_____
_____

How did I feel when I first woke today? Sluggish, tired, negative, grumpy, happy, positive.

_____
_____

How did I sleep? How many hours did I sleep for?
_____
_____

Did I dream? Nightmare? Neither?
_____
_____

Breakfast	
Lunch	
Dinner	
In-between	
drinks	

Will I do any exercise, or will I be a couch potato?

_____

What other activities will I do? Cook, clean, play with my animals, be social, create, meditate, give to others, me time, learn…

_____

Daily Reflection

Today I physically feel?

__ rested   __stressed   __sluggish

__ strong   __relaxed   __ weak

__energized   __tired   __positive

What did I do for others today?
_____
_____

What did I do for me today?
_____
_____

How do I feel emotionally?
_____
_____

Is my cup half full or half empty?
_____
_____

My affirmation for tomorrow

_____
_____
_____
_____
_____

Daily Intention   Day 17

It is my intention today to:

_____
_____

How did I feel when I first woke today? Sluggish, tired, negative, grumpy, happy, positive.

_____
_____

How did I sleep? How many hours did I sleep for?

_____
_____

Did I dream? Nightmare? Neither?

_____
_____

Breakfast	
Lunch	
Dinner	
In-between	
drinks	

Will I do any exercise, or will I be a couch potato?

_____

What other activities will I do? Cook, clean, play with my animals, be social, create, meditate, give to others, me time, learn…

_____

Daily Reflection

Today I physically feel?

__ rested __stressed __sluggish

__ strong __relaxed __ weak

__energized __tired __positive

What did I do for others today?
_____
_____

What did I do for me today?
_____
_____

How do I feel emotionally?
_____
_____

Is my cup half full or half empty?
_____
_____

My affirmation for tomorrow
_____
_____
_____
_____
_____

Daily Intention   Day 18

It is my intention today to:

_____
_____

How did I feel when I first woke today? Sluggish, tired, negative, grumpy, happy, positive.

_____
_____

How did I sleep? How many hours did I sleep for?
_____
_____

Did I dream? Nightmare? Neither?
_____
_____

Breakfast	
Lunch	
Dinner	
In-between	
drinks	

Will I do any exercise, or will I be a couch potato?

_____

What other activities will I do? Cook, clean, play with my animals, be social, create, meditate, give to others, me time, learn…

_____

Daily Reflection

Today I physically feel?

___ rested   ___stressed   ___sluggish

___ strong   ___relaxed   ___ weak

___energized   ___tired   ___positive

What did I do for others today?

_____

_____

What did I do for me today?

_____

_____

How do I feel emotionally?

_____

_____

Is my cup half full or half empty?

_____

_____

My affirmation for tomorrow

_____

_____

_____

_____

_____

Daily Intention   Day 19

It is my intention today to:

_____

_____

How did I feel when I first woke today? Sluggish, tired, negative, grumpy, happy, positive.

_____

_____

How did I sleep? How many hours did I sleep for?

_____

_____

Did I dream? Nightmare? Neither?

_____

_____

Breakfast	
Lunch	
Dinner	
In-between	
drinks	

Will I do any exercise, or will I be a couch potato?

_____

What other activities will I do? Cook, clean, play with my animals, be social, create, meditate, give to others, me time, learn…

_____

Daily Reflection

Today I physically feel?

___ rested   ___ stressed   ___ sluggish

___ strong   ___ relaxed   ___ weak

___ energized   ___ tired   ___ positive

What did I do for others today?
_____
_____

What did I do for me today?
_____
_____

How do I feel emotionally?
_____
_____

Is my cup half full or half empty?
_____
_____

My affirmation for tomorrow

_____

_____

_____

_____

_____

Daily Intention   Day 20

It is my intention today to:

_____
_____

How did I feel when I first woke today? Sluggish, tired, negative, grumpy, happy, positive.

_____
_____

How did I sleep? How many hours did I sleep for?

_____
_____

Did I dream? Nightmare? Neither?

_____
_____

Breakfast	
Lunch	
Dinner	
In-between	
drinks	

Will I do any exercise, or will I be a couch potato?

_____

What other activities will I do? Cook, clean, play with my animals, be social, create, meditate, give to others, me time, learn…

_____

Daily Reflection

Today I physically feel?

__ rested   __ stressed   __ sluggish

__ strong   __ relaxed   __ weak

__ energized   __ tired   __ positive

What did I do for others today?
_____
_____

What did I do for me today?
_____
_____

How do I feel emotionally?
_____
_____

Is my cup half full or half empty?
_____
_____

My affirmation for tomorrow
_____
_____
_____
_____

Daily Intention   Day 21

It is my intention today to:

_____
_____

How did I feel when I first woke today? Sluggish, tired, negative, grumpy, happy, positive.

_____
_____

How did I sleep? How many hours did I sleep for?
_____
_____

Did I dream? Nightmare? Neither?
_____
_____

Breakfast	
Lunch	
Dinner	
In-between	
drinks	

Will I do any exercise, or will I be a couch potato?

_____

What other activities will I do? Cook, clean, play with my animals, be social, create, meditate, give to others, me time, learn…

_____

Daily Reflection

Today I physically feel?

__ rested   __stressed   __sluggish

__ strong   __relaxed   __ weak

__energized   __tired   __positive

What did I do for others today?
_____
_____

What did I do for me today?
_____
_____

How do I feel emotionally?
_____
_____

Is my cup half full or half empty?
_____
_____

My affirmation for tomorrow

_____

_____

_____

_____

_____

Flowers bloom in their own time, each with unique colours and shapes, teaching us that growth looks different for everyone - and that patience brings beauty to life.

Daily Intention   Day 22

It is my intention today to:

_____
_____

How did I feel when I first woke today? Sluggish, tired, negative, grumpy, happy, positive.

_____
_____

How did I sleep? How many hours did I sleep for?
_____
_____

Did I dream? Nightmare? Neither?
_____
_____

Breakfast	
Lunch	
Dinner	
In-between	
drinks	

Will I do any exercise, or will I be a couch potato?

_____

What other activities will I do? Cook, clean, play with my animals, be social, create, meditate, give to others, me time, learn…

_____

Daily Reflection

Today I physically feel?

__ rested   __stressed   __sluggish

__ strong   __relaxed   __ weak

__energized   __tired   __positive

What did I do for others today?
_____
_____

What did I do for me today?
_____
_____

How do I feel emotionally?
_____
_____

Is my cup half full or half empty?
_____
_____

My affirmation for tomorrow

_____
_____
_____
_____
_____

Daily Intention   Day 23

It is my intention today to:

_____
_____

How did I feel when I first woke today? Sluggish, tired, negative, grumpy, happy, positive.

_____
_____

How did I sleep? How many hours did I sleep for?
_____
_____

Did I dream? Nightmare? Neither?
_____
_____

Breakfast	
Lunch	
Dinner	
In-between	
drinks	

Will I do any exercise, or will I be a couch potato?

_____

What other activities will I do? Cook, clean, play with my animals, be social, create, meditate, give to others, me time, learn…

_____

Daily Reflection

Today I physically feel?

__ rested   __ stressed   __ sluggish

__ strong   __ relaxed   __ weak

__ energized   __ tired   __ positive

What did I do for others today?
_____
_____

What did I do for me today?
_____
_____

How do I feel emotionally?
_____
_____

Is my cup half full or half empty?
_____
_____

My affirmation for tomorrow

_____
_____
_____
_____
_____

Daily Intention   Day 24

It is my intention today to:

_____
_____

How did I feel when I first woke today? Sluggish, tired, negative, grumpy, happy, positive.

_____
_____

How did I sleep? How many hours did I sleep for?
_____
_____

Did I dream? Nightmare? Neither?
_____
_____

Breakfast	
Lunch	
Dinner	
In-between	
drinks	

Will I do any exercise, or will I be a couch potato?

_____

What other activities will I do? Cook, clean, play with my animals, be social, create, meditate, give to others, me time, learn…

_____

Daily Reflection

Today I physically feel?

__ rested   __stressed   __sluggish

__ strong   __relaxed   __ weak

__energized   __tired   __positive

What did I do for others today?
_____
_____

What did I do for me today?
_____
_____

How do I feel emotionally?
_____
_____

Is my cup half full or half empty?
_____
_____

My affirmation for tomorrow

_____
_____
_____
_____
_____

Daily Intention   Day 25

It is my intention today to:

_____
_____

How did I feel when I first woke today? Sluggish, tired, negative, grumpy, happy, positive.

_____
_____

How did I sleep? How many hours did I sleep for?
_____
_____

Did I dream? Nightmare? Neither?
_____
_____

Breakfast	
Lunch	
Dinner	
In-between	
drinks	

Will I do any exercise, or will I be a couch potato?

_____

What other activities will I do? Cook, clean, play with my animals, be social, create, meditate, give to others, me time, learn…

_____

Daily Reflection

Today I physically feel?

__ rested   __stressed   __sluggish

__ strong   __relaxed   __ weak

__energized   __tired   __positive

What did I do for others today?
_____
_____

What did I do for me today?
_____
_____

How do I feel emotionally?
_____
_____

Is my cup half full or half empty?
_____
_____

My affirmation for tomorrow

_____
_____
_____
_____
_____

Daily Intention   Day 26

It is my intention today to:

_____
_____

How did I feel when I first woke today? Sluggish, tired, negative, grumpy, happy, positive.

_____
_____

How did I sleep? How many hours did I sleep for?
_____
_____

Did I dream? Nightmare? Neither?
_____
_____

Breakfast	
Lunch	
Dinner	
In-between	
drinks	

Will I do any exercise, or will I be a couch potato?

_____

What other activities will I do? Cook, clean, play with my animals, be social, create, meditate, give to others, me time, learn...

_____

Daily Reflection

Today I physically feel?

__ rested   __ stressed   __ sluggish

__ strong   __ relaxed   __ weak

__ energized   __ tired   __ positive

What did I do for others today?
_____
_____

What did I do for me today?
_____
_____

How do I feel emotionally?
_____
_____

Is my cup half full or half empty?
_____
_____

My affirmation for tomorrow

_____
_____
_____
_____
_____

Daily Intention   Day 27

It is my intention today to:

_____
_____

How did I feel when I first woke today? Sluggish, tired, negative, grumpy, happy, positive.

_____
_____

How did I sleep? How many hours did I sleep for?
_____
_____

Did I dream? Nightmare? Neither?
_____
_____

Breakfast	
Lunch	
Dinner	
In-between	
drinks	

Will I do any exercise, or will I be a couch potato?

_____

What other activities will I do? Cook, clean, play with my animals, be social, create, meditate, give to others, me time, learn…

_____

Daily Reflection

Today I physically feel?

__ rested   __ stressed   __ sluggish

__ strong   __ relaxed   __ weak

__ energized   __ tired   __ positive

What did I do for others today?
_____
_____

What did I do for me today?
_____
_____

How do I feel emotionally?
_____
_____

Is my cup half full or half empty?
_____
_____

My affirmation for tomorrow

_____
_____
_____
_____
_____

Daily Intention   Day 28

It is my intention today to:

_____
_____

How did I feel when I first woke today? Sluggish, tired, negative, grumpy, happy, positive.

_____
_____

How did I sleep? How many hours did I sleep for?
_____
_____

Did I dream? Nightmare? Neither?
_____
_____

Breakfast	
Lunch	
Dinner	
In-between	
drinks	

Will I do any exercise, or will I be a couch potato?

_____

What other activities will I do? Cook, clean, play with my animals, be social, create, meditate, give to others, me time, learn...

_____

Daily Reflection

Today I physically feel?

__ rested   __stressed   __sluggish

__ strong   __relaxed   __ weak

__energized   __tired   __positive

What did I do for others today?

_____

_____

What did I do for me today?

_____

_____

How do I feel emotionally?

_____

_____

Is my cup half full or half empty?

_____

_____

My affirmation for tomorrow

_____

_____

_____

_____

_____

Daily Intention   Day 29

It is my intention today to:

_____
_____

How did I feel when I first woke today? Sluggish, tired, negative, grumpy, happy, positive.

_____
_____

How did I sleep? How many hours did I sleep for?
_____
_____

Did I dream? Nightmare? Neither?
_____
_____

Breakfast	
Lunch	
Dinner	
In-between	
drinks	

Will I do any exercise, or will I be a couch potato?

_____

What other activities will I do? Cook, clean, play with my animals, be social, create, meditate, give to others, me time, learn…

_____

Daily Reflection

Today I physically feel?

__ rested   __stressed   __sluggish

__ strong   __relaxed   __ weak

__energized   __tired   __positive

What did I do for others today?
_____
_____

What did I do for me today?
_____
_____

How do I feel emotionally?
_____
_____

Is my cup half full or half empty?
_____
_____

My affirmation for tomorrow

_____

_____

_____

_____

_____

Daily Intention   Day 30

It is my intention today to:

_____
_____

How did I feel when I first woke today? Sluggish, tired, negative, grumpy, happy, positive.

_____
_____

How did I sleep? How many hours did I sleep for?

_____
_____

Did I dream? Nightmare? Neither?

_____
_____

Breakfast	
Lunch	
Dinner	
In-between	
drinks	

Will I do any exercise, or will I be a couch potato?

_____

What other activities will I do? Cook, clean, play with my animals, be social, create, meditate, give to others, me time, learn...

_____

Daily Reflection

Today I physically feel?

__ rested   __stressed   __sluggish

__ strong   __relaxed   __ weak

__energized   __tired   __positive

What did I do for others today?

_____

_____

What did I do for me today?

_____

_____

How do I feel emotionally?

_____

_____

Is my cup half full or half empty?

_____

_____

My affirmation for tomorrow

_____

_____

_____

_____

_____

Daily Intention   Day 31

It is my intention today to:

_____
_____

How did I feel when I first woke today? Sluggish, tired, negative, grumpy, happy, positive.

_____
_____

How did I sleep? How many hours did I sleep for?

_____
_____

Did I dream? Nightmare? Neither?

_____
_____

Breakfast	
Lunch	
Dinner	
In-between drinks	

Will I do any exercise, or will I be a couch potato?

_____

What other activities will I do? Cook, clean, play with my animals, be social, create, meditate, give to others, me time, learn…

_____

Daily Reflection

Today I physically feel?

__ rested   __ stressed   __ sluggish

__ strong   __ relaxed   __ weak

__ energized   __ tired   __ positive

What did I do for others today?
_____
_____

What did I do for me today?
_____
_____

How do I feel emotionally?
_____
_____

Is my cup half full or half empty?
_____
_____

My affirmation for tomorrow

_____

_____

_____

_____

_____

Now you have been setting intentions and doing daily reflections for 31 days, how are you feeling emotionally and physically?

Can you see any patterns emerging?

I am proud of you for coming this far.

Are YOU proud of YOU?

Write down your immediate thoughts.

Don't overthink it.

_____

_____

_____

_____

_____

_____

_____

_____

_____

_____

THINKING ABOUT THE PATTERNS YOU HAVE

REFLECTED ON,

CONSIDER WHAT IT IS YOU ARE GOING TO DO TO

HONOUR

YOUR

HEART

I commit to doing more of:

_____

_____

_____

_____

_____

_____

_____

_____

_____

_____

_____

_____

_____

_____

I commit to doing less of:

In your commitment to yourself,
allow space for nurturing your spiritual side.
On the opposite page, I've listed what I personally do for me.
Make a list of what you can do for you.

Think about all that interests you and who,
or what, can support you on your journey.
How can learning about this support you back to being you?

What is it that you love that will nurture your soul
and help your energy to flow again?

I want to learn more about:

_____
_____
_____
_____
_____
_____
_____
_____
_____
_____
_____
_____
_____

Gaps may seem like empty spaces, but they remind us that pauses and open moments allow room for growth, connection, and a fresh perspective.

It's important that you do learn to honour your spiritual side –
whatever that may be for you.

It's our knowing, that gut feeling,
the sixth sense that we all need to honour.
Honouring our spiritual side is surrendering to who we really are
and accepting what is and what will be.

It allows us grace and to flow in life with gratitude.

Explore what you want to learn about. Continuously.
Research and practice it. The more you practice
what you learn the more awareness you will
have. Meditate and become **mindful**,
not mind full.

This journal has come to an end but for you its just the beginning.

Reflect on your notes, summarise what you have learned.

Set priorities for yourself and make them very clear not only to yourself, but to those around you.

What are you going to leave behind?

Let go of?

Get rid of all negative patterns – emotionally and physically that occur in your life.

What are you going to do more of?

For you and only you?

Create new patterns for you.

What have you committed to?

Begin today. Not tomorrow. Not next week. Not next month.

Your future to

Honouring Your Heart

begins

now.

Lessons are like lamp posts, standing quietly on the edges of the night, reminding us that even in the darkest moments, a little light can lead the way.

About the Photographer

Talented young Australian photographer based in Brisbane, Georgia is neurodivergent and has a passion for capturing the world through her lens. With a Certificate III in Photography from TAFE Queensland, she specialises in product photography, bringing a unique perspective and creativity to her work. When she's not behind the camera, you can find Georgia exploring local op shops for hidden treasures or enjoying her favourite K-pop tunes alongside her crazy dog. With an eye for detail and a love for storytelling, Georgia is excited to continue her journey in photography and share her vision with the world.

Copyright © 2024 Daisy Lane Publishing
First published in Australia in 2024
By Daisy Lane Publishing/Daisy Lane Inspirational
https://www.daisylanepublishing.com

All rights reserved. No part of this publication may be reproduced, distributed or transmitted in any form or by any means, graphic, electronic, or mechanical, including photocopying, recording, taping, or by any other information storage retrieval system the written permission of the copyright owner except in the case of brief quotations embodied in critical articles and reviews.

Because of the dynamic nature of the internet, any web addresses or links contained in this book may have changed since publication and may no longer be valid. The views expressed in this work are solely those of the author and do not necessarily reflect the views of the publisher and the publisher hereby disclaims any responsibility for them.

 A catalogue record for this work is available from the National Library of Australia

National library of Australia Catalogue-In-Publication data:

Life In Line/Georgia Worthington and Jennifer Sharp

Book Cover Art © 2024 Georgia Worthington
Internal Images © 2024 Georgia Worthington
Edited by Michelle Worthington

ISBN: (SC) 978-1-7-6367004-4

www.ingramcontent.com/pod-product-compliance
Lightning Source LLC
Chambersburg PA
CBHW042226090526
44585CB00001BA/6